Published in the United States
by Potter Style, an imprint of the
Crown Publishing Group, a division
of Random House, Inc., New York.
Potter Style is a trademark and
Potter with colophon is a registered
trademark of Random House, Inc.

ISBN 978-0-385-34498-2

Photos by Laurel Golio
Cover and interior design by
    Danielle Deschenes
Styled by Natalia Moena

Interior patterns from Shutterstock
.com © Kostiantyn Ablazov (pp.
2–3); © Arkady Mazor (pp. 68–69);
© Paul Cowan (pp. 112–13); © sootra
(pp. 122–23)

www.potterstyle.com
Printed in China

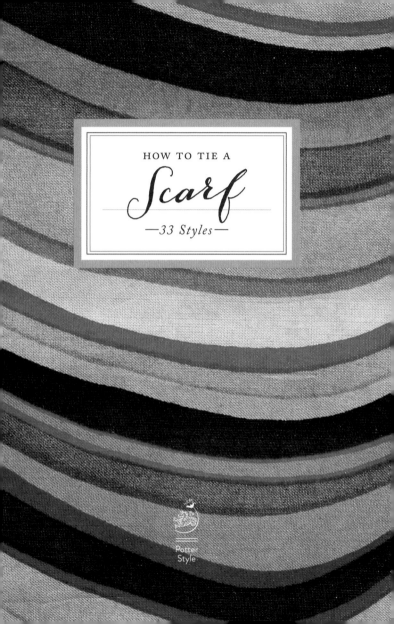

HOW TO TIE A

Scarf

—*33 Styles*—

Potter
Style

Contents

Introduction

In the lexicon of fashion accessories, scarves possess the unique ability to endure passing trends and define individual style.

Large statement scarves with elegant prints, chunky-knit scarves woven with multicolored yarn, intricate crocheted capes with fringe detail, delicate pocket scarves in raw silk; the variety of shapes, patterns, and materials are limited only to the imagination of the designer.

With the endless variety of modern and vintage scarves available, there are even more ways to style them. *How to Tie a Scarf* provides an introduction to wearing your scarves in classic and inventive ways. In these pages—divided among basic folds, common shapes, seasonal and embellished scarves sections— you'll find thirty-three ways to twist, knot, and loop your scarves expertly and effortlessly.

Consider this your invitation to reintroduce older pieces in your wardrobe with a fresh perspective and wear your new scarves with an unexpected twist. No matter the fashion, as Chanel famously quipped, good style always endures.

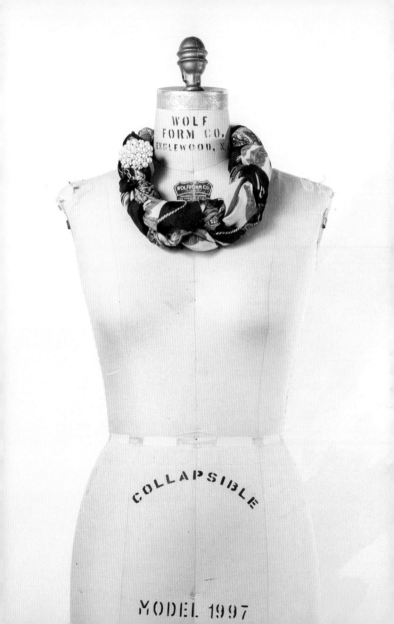

CHAPTER 1

Fold & Pleat

—*Begin with the Basics*—

Four Essential Folds

Many of the styles featured in this book begin with one of four basic folds:
The Bias, The Bandanna, The Straight, and The Triangle. These techniques
are primarily useful when folding square scarves into oblong bands, but they
also serve as the foundation for several oblong scarves for the colder months.
Use these simple folds as a starting point when styling your scarves.

—The Triangle Fold—

⊨ STEP ONE ⊨

BEGIN with an open scarf.

⊨ STEP TWO ⊨

FOLD the scarf diagonally in
half to form a triangle.

—The Straight Fold—

STEP ONE

BEGIN with an open scarf.

STEP TWO

FOLD the scarf in half lengthwise.

STEP THREE

CONTINUE folding the scarf lengthwise until the desired width is achieved.

—The Bandanna Fold—

STEP ONE

FOLD the scarf diagonally in half.

STEP TWO

TAKE the triangular corner of the scarf and fold inward toward the middle, leaving two-thirds of the scarf unfolded.

STEP THREE

TAKE the opposite side of the scarf and fold inward toward the folded corner.

STEP FOUR

KEEP folding the alternate sides of the scarf until the desired width is achieved.

➤➤ TIP *You can create a classic bandanna if you tie this fold around the neck, or a simple headband if you use a light silk or chiffon scarf.*

—The Bias Fold—

⊢ STEP ONE ⊢

TAKE the opposite corners of the scarf and fold inward toward the center of the scarf.

⊢ STEP TWO ⊢

CONTINUE folding-in the opposite sides in thirds.

⊢ STEP THREE ⊢

FINISH folding when the scarf is a two-inch band. Flip the scarf so that the folds are hidden.

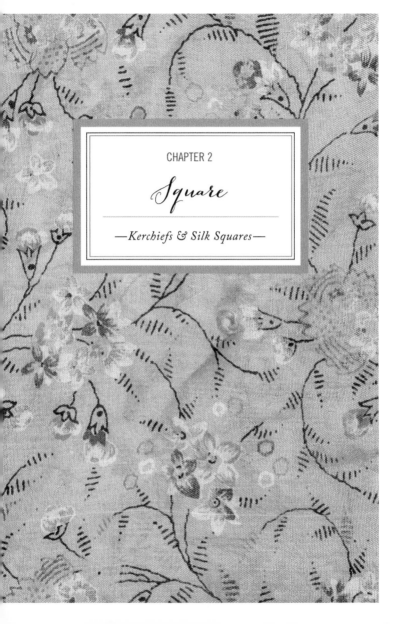

CHAPTER 2

Square

—*Kerchiefs & Silk Squares*—

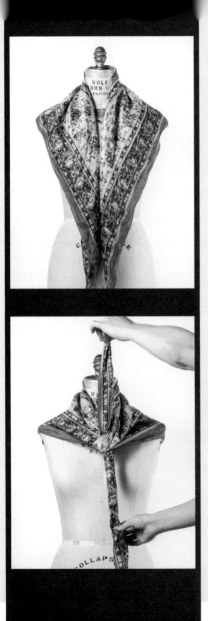

BEGIN with the triangle fold. Drape the scarf around the neck, allowing both ends to hang evenly in front of the chest.

CROSS the ends of the scarf at the base of the neck and pull in the opposite direction.

⫸ STEP THREE ⫷

KNOT the ends of the scarf together to secure at the base.

⇥ TIP *The Nantucket can be styled using a light silk or chiffon scarf for the summer months, ideally complementing a V-neck blouse or T-shirt. When the weather requires a light jacket, use a thicker scarf underneath for a bit of additional warmth and a tiny peek of color and pattern.*

the Marrakech

➤➤ TIP *An everyday effortless style, the Marrakech looks best with a simple T-shirt and jeans. Use a square scarf made of light cotton, linen, or silk to achieve this draped look—anything heavier will bulk.*

⊣ STEP ONE ⊢

BEGIN with the triangle fold. Lay the triangle facing forward on your body with the tips of the scarf resting on the back.

⊣ STEP TWO ⊢

CROSS the ends of the scarf in the back, then bring them forward so that they are resting on your chest, lying on either side of the triangle.

WOLF
FORM CO.
EWOOD

WOLFORM

SHERRON
MISSY

the Cannes

COLLAPSIBLE

⟹ STEP ONE ⊨

BEGIN with the bandanna fold. Drape the scarf around the neck, allowing both ends to hang evenly in front of the chest.

⟹ STEP TWO ⊨

CROSS the ends of the scarf. Twist and pull both ends in the opposite direction.

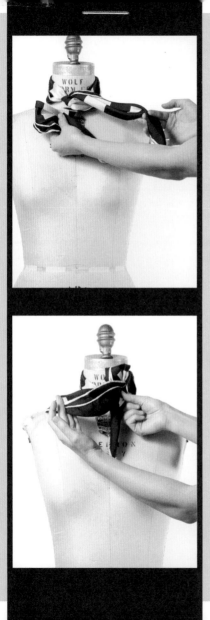

⊨ STEP THREE ⊨

CREATE a loop with one end of the scarf, close to the neck.

⊨ STEP FOUR ⊨

CROSS the opposite end of the scarf around the loop, keeping both ends taut.

⟹ STEP FIVE ⟸

PULL the opposite end of
the scarf through the loop
and tighten into a bow.
Adjust the ends so that
they appear even.

➤➤ TIP *Beaucoup femme and
just the right amount of
fussy, The Cannes is perfect
for both a romantic or pro-
fessional look, depending on
the choice of print and material. With a classic striped
silk, match this style with a
blazer or cable-knit sweater
for the office. This knot sits
beautifully above a round-
neck or bateau blouse.*

the *Surrey*

⟩ STEP ONE ⟨

BEGIN with the triangle fold. Drape the scarf around the neck, with the ends hanging evenly on the back and the front of the scarf centered on the chest. Begin to pull one end of the scarf around to the front.

⟩ STEP TWO ⟨

PULL the opposite end of the scarf toward the front.

⊨ STEP THREE ⊨

TIE the ends of the scarf together in a tight knot over the front of the scarf, at the base of the neck. Adjust to either side and pull the bottom layer out slightly, depending on preference.

➤➤ TIP *The Surrey is best suited for colder months, when it can be tucked under a jacket or heavy sweater. A quilted Barbour coat is a classic match with the herringbone pattern featured in the tutorial, but could also be updated with a jersey top and a modern geometric-patterned scarf.*

the Montmartre

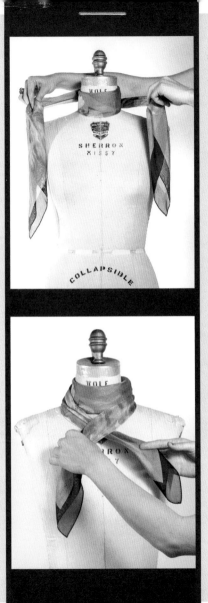

⟹ STEP ONE ⟸

USE the bias fold to begin. Position the scarf in the center of your neck and wrap the ends around, crossing them behind your neck and then pulling forward.

⟹ STEP TWO ⟸

BRING the ends together in front, crossing them at the base of the neck.

TIE one knot in the center of the scarf, pulling the ends in opposite directions.

DOUBLE-KNOT the scarf and let the ends hang loosely. Twist the knot to one side of your neck so that it rests slightly off-center.

➤➤ TIP *This classic style pays homage to iconic Parisian chic. Worn in the spring, summer, and early fall, the Montmartre looks best with bateau tops and blouses.*

the Jackson Hole

COLLAPSIBLE

MODEL 1997

⊨ STEP ONE ⊨

BEGIN with the triangle fold.
Drape it around the neck,
with both ends hanging
evenly on the back.

⊨ STEP TWO ⊨

TIE the ends of the scarf
and secure with a double
knot. Adjust the scarf so
that it rests on the center
of the chest.

➤➤ TIP *Ideal for casual
sportswear, this style can
be worn in a variety of
prints and materials for a
simple, utilitarian look.*

═══╡ STEP ONE ╞═══

BEGIN a basic bandanna
fold, stopping one step
before completing it.
Allow the triangular edge
to remain unfolded.

═══╡ STEP TWO ╞═══

WRAP the scarf around the
neck, with the ends hanging
evenly on the back and the
triangular edge centered on
the chest.

═══╡ STEP THREE ╞═══

TIE the ends of the scarf
together in a square knot
at the back of the neck and
adjust the front triangular
edge slightly to one side.

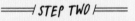

STEP ONE

BEGIN with a large light-weight silk scarf and fold into a triangle. Drape around the neck with the ends hanging evenly on the back and the front centered on the chest.

STEP TWO

TIE the ends of the scarf into a loose knot. Pull the scarf down from the front of the neck and spread it across the chest to maximize the chiffon material and achieve a fuller look.

The Mission

STEP ONE

BEGIN with a large embellished scarf (lined and with tassels is best here) and fold into a triangle. Drape around the neck with the ends hanging evenly on the back and the front centered on the chest.

STEP TWO

TIE the ends of the scarf into a loose knot. Adjust the scarf to the side so that the triangular portion lies on the hip.

STEP THREE

PULL the scarf from the base of the neck toward the shoulder and the bottom layer outward to create a layered look and to highlight the embellished edges.

CHAPTER 3

Oblong

—*Skinny & Wide*—

the Geneva

➤➤ TIP *Both long and short scarves work for this style, depending on how many times the scarf is wrapped around the neck. Choose shorter, lighter scarves for the summer, and longer, heavier scarves to keep you warm in the winter.*

STEP ONE

BEGIN with a straight fold. Wrap the scarf once around the neck, allowing one end to hang approximately three-fourths longer in the front than the other end.

STEP TWO

WRAP the longer end of the scarf securely around the neck a second time and tuck it under the wrapped portion in the back. Wrap the loose end in the front around around the neck and tuck in tightly.

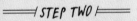

tuck end in here

STEP ONE

DRAPE the scarf around the neck, allowing both ends to hang evenly in the front.

➤ TIP *Use an elaborately patterned or interestingly textured scarf for this style—looping the scarf around the neck several times will highlight the various colors and inter-woven materials.*

═══ STEP TWO ═══

WRAP the shorter end of
the scarf loosely around
the neck.

═══ STEP THREE ═══

BEGIN to loop the opposite
end around the front por-
tion of the scarf.

╪ STEP FOUR ╪

PULL through and continue to tightly loop the opposite end around the front portion of the scarf.

╪ STEP FIVE ╪

WHEN the end of the scarf is almost completely wrapped around the front, pull the remaining end toward the back and tie both ends together.

the Madison Ave.

=====| STEP ONE |=====

DRAPE the scarf around the neck, allowing both ends to hang evenly in the front.

➤➤ TIP *The Madison Ave. is a bold style—one that can look romantic as shown in a lace pattern or preppy in a herringbone or equestrian pattern. Pair this with a simple A-line dress, with the bow serving as your statement piece.*

CROSS the ends of the scarf loosely below the bust.

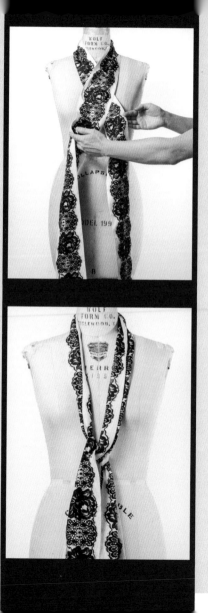

CROSS the ends and pull one end over the other to tie a single knot loosely.

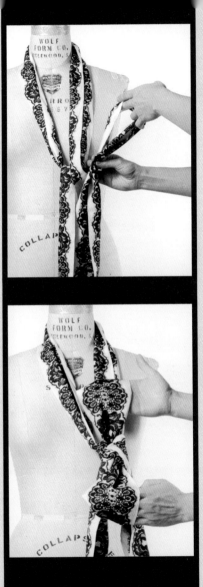

CREATE a loop with one end
of the scarf.

CROSS the left end of the
scarf around the loop,
keeping both ends taut
and tie into a bow.

➤➤ TIP *If you use a short scarf and keep the rolled knot close to the neck, this style can be used for warmth or as a sweatband while hiking or trekking. When using a long scarf (as illustrated in the example), the rolled knot sits above the bust as a necklace.*

=| STEP ONE |=

BEGIN with the straight fold. Drape the scarf around the neck, allowing both ends to hang evenly in the front.

=== STEP TWO ===

CROSS the ends of the scarf at the base of the neck.

=== STEP THREE ===

TIE the ends loosely together, approximately two inches below the neck.

wrap and
tuck end in

tuck
end
in
here

=/ STEP FOUR /=

WRAP one end tightly around
the center of the tied scarf
and tuck the end back into
the wrap.

=/ STEP FIVE /=

REPEAT on the opposite
side, keeping the end as
tight as possible. Adjust
as needed.

the Greenwich

➤➤ TIP *This classic style looks best under a peacoat or winter jacket, with the top knot peeking out for additional color.*

=== STEP ONE ===

DRAPE the scarf around the neck, allowing one end to hang one-third longer than the other in the front.

STEP TWO

WRAP the longer end of the scarf loosely around the neck.

STEP THREE

CONTINUE wrapping the longer end of the scarf around the neck until it lies on the front of the chest.

CROSS the ends of the scarf under the wrapped portion at the base of the neck.

PULL one end of the scarf through, creating a knot. Loosen and pull the wrapped portion of the scarf over the knot to hide it.

the *Stockholm*

COLLAPSIBLE

MODEL 1997

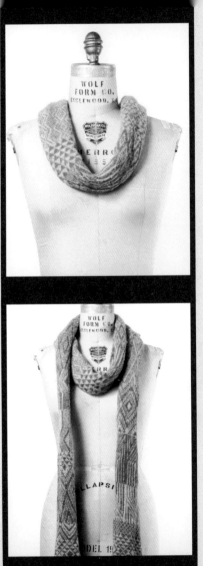

═══┤ STEP ONE ├═══

DRAPE the scarf around the neck, allowing both ends to hang evenly in the back.

═══┤ STEP TWO ├═══

CROSS the ends behind your back and then pull them forward so that they rest evenly on the chest.

⟾ STEP THREE ⟾

BEGIN to wrap one end
around the initial loop of
the scarf.

=== STEP FOUR ==

PULL through and continue to wrap one end around the initial loop. Once this is complete, tuck the remaining end of the scarf into the back of the neck.

=== STEP FIVE ==

REPEAT with the opposite end of the scarf.

➤➤ TIP *The Copenhagen's northern cousin, The Stockholm is best worn in a heavy material for chillier weather.*

the Hanoi

➤➤ TIP *The Hanoi is an intricate style and needs adequate room to display its multiple loops. Use a light linen, silk, or even chiffon scarf (knits and heavier materials aren't as malleable and will overwhelm the detail) when creating this look.*

⊨ STEP ONE ⊨

DRAPE the scarf around the neck, allowing one end to hang slightly longer than the other in the front.

⊨ STEP TWO ⊨

CROSS the longer end of the scarf over the shorter one at the base of the neck.

STEP THREE

PULL the longer end of the scarf through to tie loosely.

STEP FOUR

TAKE the end you just pulled through (approximately two inches below the knot) and cross over the other end again. Pull under and through to create a second knot.

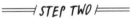

STEP ONE

FOLD the scarf in half lengthwise. Wrap the scarf around the neck, allowing both loose ends to rest on the side of one shoulder and the folded loop to rest on the other.

STEP TWO

PULL one end of the scarf through the folded loop in the front.

STEP THREE

TIE the remaining end loosely around the opposite end, allowing both to hang evenly on the front of the chest.

=== STEP ONE ===

BEGIN with a straight fold. Wrap the scarf around the neck with the ends facing forward, one one-third longer than the other.

➤➤ TIP *The Mayfair works beautifully tucked beneath a light jacket or a cardigan in temperate climates. A long, rectangular neck scarf is ideal for this style; make sure to use a light to medium-heavy material (cotton, linen, silk, thin wool, cashmere), otherwise it will be difficult to tie the knot.*

⊨ STEP TWO ⊨

TIE a knot in the middle of
the longer end.

⊨ STEP THREE ⊨

PULL the end to tighten the
knot.

═══ STEP FOUR ═══

PULL the loose end of the scarf through the knot.

═══ STEP FIVE ═══

PULL the knot upward to tighten. Position the knot in the center of your neck, with the ends flowing over the front of your chest.

CHAPTER 4

Embellished

—*Sequined, Ruffled & Tasseled*—

the Picadilly

➤➤ TIP *You can also use a monochromatic ruffled scarf to blend with a variety of jackets, blouses, and dresses.*

STEP ONE

BEGIN with a ruffled oblong scarf and drape it around the base of the neck so that both ends hang evenly in the back. Wrap each end around and toward the front, then tuck the remaining ends into the scarf.

STEP ONE

BEGIN with an oblong scarf embellished with sequins. Drape the scarf around the neck, allowing one end to hang slightly longer than the other in the front. Wrap the longer end loosely around the neck, allowing the opposite end to remain in the front.

➤➤ TIP *The Palm Springs is a fun and flashy evening style, best worn for special occasions in warmer climates (you wouldn't want to hide the sequins with a jacket, would you?).*

The Palm Beach

═══╡ STEP ONE ╞═══

DRAPE the scarf around the neck, allowing one end to hang slightly longer than the other in the front.

═══╡ STEP TWO ╞═══

CROSS both ends of the scarf at the base of the neck.

═══╡ STEP THREE ╞═══

PULL the longer end of the scarf through to tie loosely.

The Palm Desert

⫽ STEP ONE ⫽

DRAPE the scarf around the neck, allowing both ends to hang evenly in the back.

⫽ STEP TWO ⫽

FAN out the scarf in the front, so that the material rests across the shoulders.

STEP ONE

BEGIN by folding a fringed square lace scarf into the triangle fold. Drape across one side of the chest so that the triangular portion of the scarf rests on the hip and the ends hang on the back.

STEP TWO

PULL one end of the scarf forward so that it rests on the opposite side of the chest.

➤➤ TIP *A shocking-red shawl is more Stevie Nicks than Betty White, and this version in black would be a perfect complement for an evening dress.*

➤➤ TIP *When styling a scarf with pom-poms or other trimmings that line the edges, creating a layered look that displays the embellishments (like the Oslo and its following variations) is ideal. Keep the rest of your outfit relatively simple; you don't want to overwhelm or detract from the embellishments on the scarf.*

⟩ STEP ONE ⟨

BEGIN by folding an oblong
scarf embellished with
pom-poms in half. Drape
loosely across the chest,
with both ends hanging in
the back and one end much
shorter than the other.

⟞ STEP TWO ⟝

WRAP the longer end around the back of the neck.

⟞ STEP THREE ⟝

PULL the longer end of the scarf forward and wrap it loosely around the neck, slightly on top of the first layer.

STEP FOUR

KEEP wrapping and layering the scarf until only a small portion remains.

STEP FIVE

TUCK the remaining end of the scarf into the front and the opposite end into the back, hidden in the folds. Adjust the front layers so that the pom-poms are evenly spaced.

FOLD the scarf in half and adjust so that both layers of pom-poms are visible.

DRAPE the scarf around the neck, allowing both ends to hang evenly in the back.

FAN out the scarf in the front so that the material rests evenly across the shoulders.

The Trondheim

STEP ONE

FOLD the scarf in half and adjust so both layers of pom-poms are visible.

STEP TWO

DRAPE the scarf around the neck, allowing one end to hang slightly longer than the other in the back.

STEP THREE

PULL both ends forward to rest on the front of the chest.

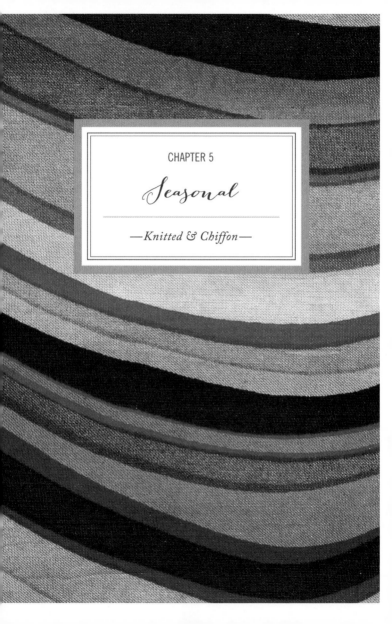

CHAPTER 5

Seasonal

—Knitted & Chiffon—

SHERRON
MISSY

the Southampton

—*Summer Style*—

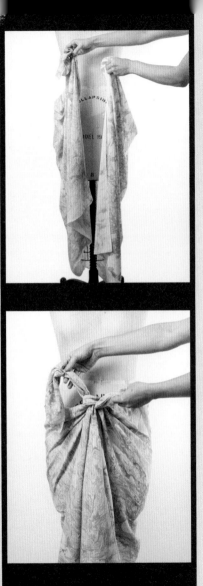

STEP ONE

FOLD an oversize oblong scarf in half. Wrap around the hips and pull the top ends forward.

STEP TWO

CENTER and tie the ends together, slightly below the hips.

═══╡ STEP THREE ╞═══

TAKE the bottom hem of the scarf and pull upward.

═══╡ STEP FOUR ╞═══

TIE the bottom ends of the scarf together. Tuck the knot behind the upper ends of the scarf, and adjust accordingly.

➤➤ TIP *As the name implies, the Southampton is perfect for the beach or poolside lounging. Sarongs come in a surprising range of prints and colors—they are a great way to introduce pattern into your summer wardrobe.*

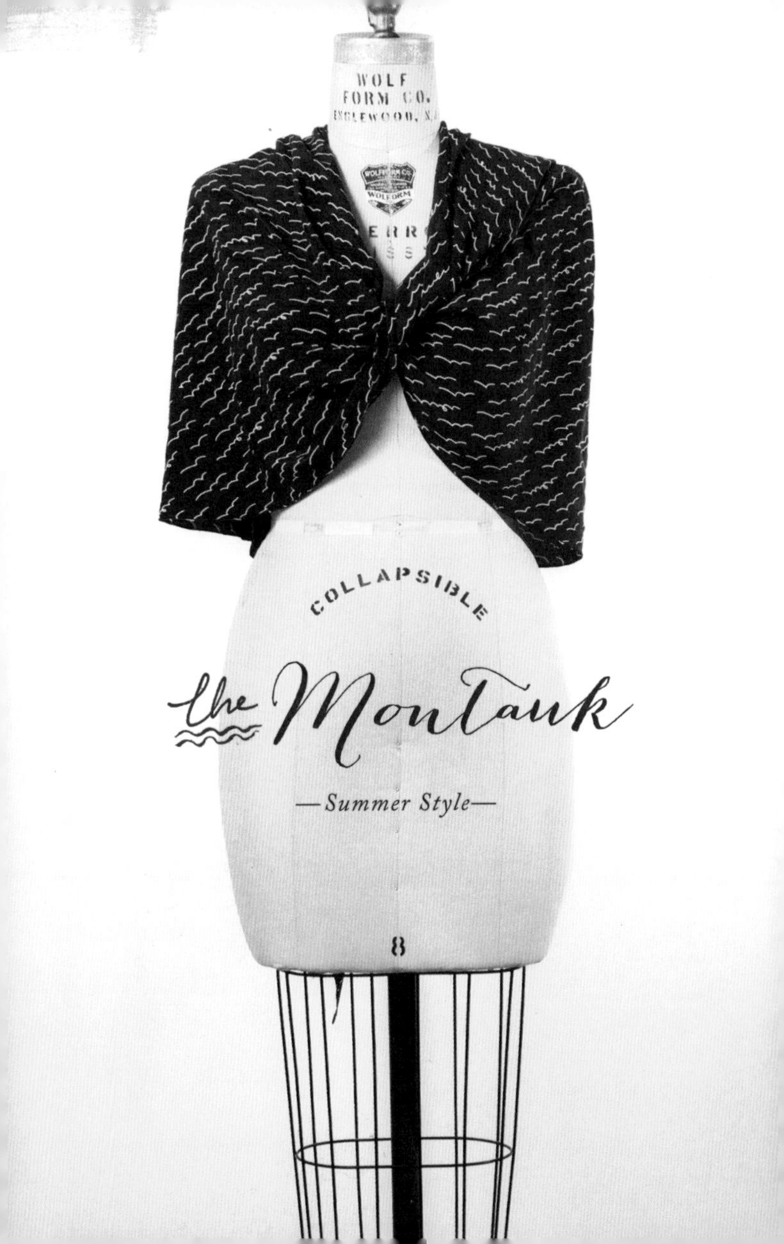

the Montauk

—*Summer Style*—

══╡ STEP ONE ╞══

DRAPE one end of a wide oblong scarf over one shoulder. Make a single twist in the center of the chest.

══╡ STEP TWO ╞══

DRAPE the opposite end of the scarf over the other shoulder.

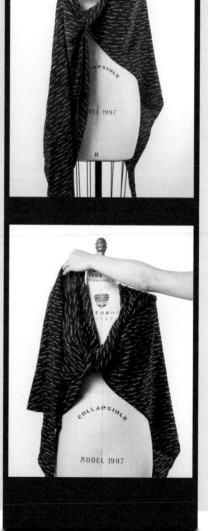

⊨ STEP THREE ⊨

(BACK VIEW): TIE both ends together in a loose knot at the lower back.

➤➤ TIP *Wear the Montauk with a strapless dress or strappy camisole in the summer. It's perfect in a light nautical print for day or a deep purple chiffon for evening.*

the *Kashmir*

—*Fall Style*—

➤➤ TIP *Evocative of the raw beauty of the mountains in Kashmir, this scarf wraps close to the neck and is meant to be worn in higher altitudes or colder climates.*

⸗∣ STEP ONE ∣⸗

DRAPE the scarf around the neck, allowing both ends to hang evenly in the back. Adjust the front so that the scarf wraps slightly wider on the left shoulder.

⸗∣ STEP TWO ∣⸗

PULL the right end of the scarf over the front of the chest.

WRAP the right end of the scarf around the right shoulder, fanning the end of the scarf out to display the fringe evenly.

PULL the left end of the scarf over the right shoulder. Wrap the left end of the scarf around the neck, then adjust it so that the right side of the scarf can be seen. Tuck any loose ends into the back of the neck.

The Jammu

STEP ONE

WRAP one end of the scarf over the left shoulder, with the bottom of the scarf sitting on the hip.

STEP TWO

WRAP the remaining material over the right shoulder, around the front of the neck, and over the left shoulder.

STEP THREE

PULL the scarf slightly down from the base of the neck and roll.

The Rajouri

STEP ONE

BEGIN with the straight fold. Drape the scarf around the neck, allowing both ends to hang evenly in the front.

STEP TWO

TAKE one end of the scarf and wrap it completely around the neck so that it rests on the front of the chest.

STEP THREE

TAKE the opposite end of the scarf and wrap it around the neck, then it tuck into the back.

the Dorchester

—Fall Style—

⊨ STEP ONE ⊨

FOLD the scarf in half to create a loop on one end of the scarf. Drape the scarf over the neck, pulling the loop to one side and allowing the ends to lie on the opposite side of the chest.

⊨ STEP TWO ⊨

PULL the ends through the loop. Tighten the loop and adjust to the side of the chest.

➤➤TIP *This simple, classic knot works with most oblong scarves and can be worn in a variety of ways, depending on the material. As styled above, the Dorchester is ideal for fall, tucked under a rain jacket or light peacoat.*

the *Kyoto*

—Fall Style—

=== | STEP ONE | ===

PULL the ends of a large
oblong silk scarf over the
shoulders, resting them
evenly on the hips.

=== | STEP TWO | ===

TIE the right back corner of
the scarf to the front right
corner in a tight knot.

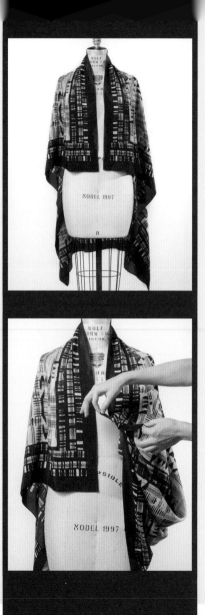

STEP THREE

REPEAT with the left corner.

STEP FOUR

FASTEN both tied corners with a brooch (hiding the knots) and securing the scarf in place.

>> TIP *Evocative of exquisite Japanese kimonos, the Kyoto can be worn in place of a jacket during the spring.*

the *Edinburgh*

—Winter Style—

➤➤ TIP *An oversize plaid wool scarf is a winter staple. Wool provides warmth during the colder months, and plaid is easy to match with most outerwear. The above style can be worn both indoors and out, while the final look in the series (the St. Andrews) works as a stylish half-jacket.*

⟩ STEP ONE ⟨

FOLD the scarf in half and loosely drape the ends over the shoulders so that both ends hang evenly in the back.

STEP ONE

FOLD the scarf in half and wrap around the neck so that both ends hang evenly in the front of the chest.

STEP TWO

CROSS both ends at the center of the neck and loosely pull them to rest on the back.

STEP THREE

PULL the back of the scarf upward to create a half hood.

COLLAPSIBLE

MODEL 1997

The St. Andrews

STEP ONE

FOLD the scarf in half and wrap it around the shoulders, allowing both ends to hang evenly in the front of the chest.

STEP TWO

BEGINNING at the base of the neck and running down to the bottom, fold the scarf over two inches.

STEP THREE

CROSS the right side of the scarf across the chest, lining up the plaid evenly.

STEP FOUR

FASTEN a brooch directly under the collar, pinning the scarf in place.

the Lahore

—Winter Style—

➤➤ TIP *A pashmina is another winter essential that can be worn multiple ways. Try wrapping it around the neck, wearing it as a loose shawl, or even pulling it over the head to wear in place of a hat.*

=== STEP ONE ===

DRAPE a large pashmina around the neck, allowing one end to hang slightly longer than the other. Wrap the longer end loosely around the neck, with the opposite side remaining in front.

the Tokyo

—Spring Style—

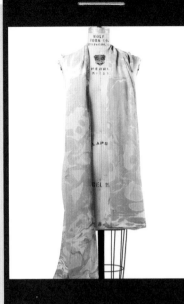

STEP ONE

DRAPE an oblong silk scarf around the neck, allowing one end to hang slightly longer on the chest.

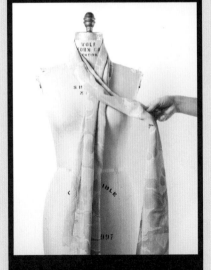

STEP TWO

TAKE the longer end and cross it over the shorter end at the base of the neck.

=== STEP THREE |===

PULL the longer end of the scarf through at the base of the neck. Pull the longer end of the scarf halfway through the knot.

⊨ STEP FOUR ⊨

HOLD the loop and pull
downward, so that the
hanging end moves up
and the middle tier moves
down. Adjust to make all
three tiers stack evenly.

➤➤ TIP *This style can be worn
under a light trench coat and
rain jacket. Seemingly com-
plex, these waterfall ruffles
are easily achieved and add
additional texture and layers to otherwise monotonous
rainy-day outfits.*

↓ pull
middle
loop
down

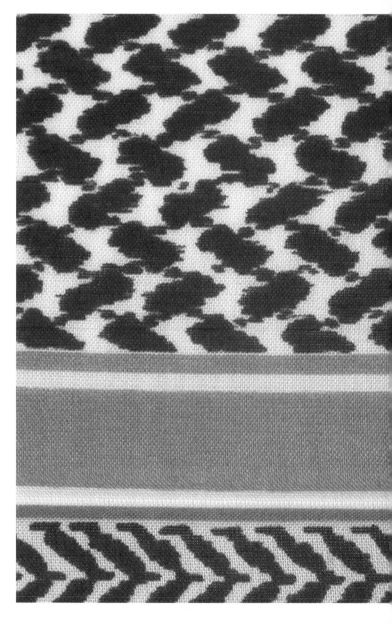

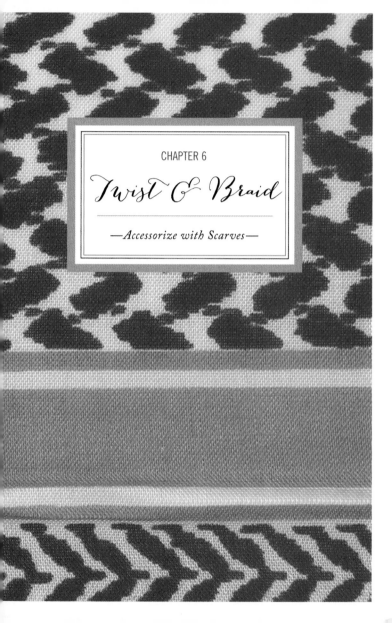

CHAPTER 6

Twist & Braid

—Accessorize with Scarves—

The SoHo Camera Strap

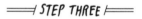

STEP ONE

WRAP a skinny silk scarf around the neck.

STEP TWO

THREAD one end of the scarf through the side of the camera (where its original straps were attached).

STEP THREE

REPEAT on the opposite side.

STEP FOUR

PULL the ends upward to adjust where the camera will sit on the body.

STEP FIVE

SECURE the strap by tying the loose ends into a tight knot on both sides.

➤➤ TIP *Secure this strap permanently by attaching key rings to the ends of the scarf. For a more polished look, consider sewing leather bands around each end.*

The Uptown Tote

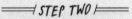

STEP ONE

TIE the opposite corners of a square silk scarf together. The space beneath this knot represents the body of the tote, so adjust for room as desired.

STEP TWO

PULL the remaining corners upward and tie together. Allow enough space between the first and second knot to fit over the shoulder.

➤ TIP *Play with a variety of sizes to create larger or smaller purses—a sarong is a great choice for a casual beach tote.*

The Williamsburg Laces

⊨ STEP ONE ⊨

UNLACE a pair of leather sneakers or boots—ideally choose a pair that require short laces.

⊨ STEP TWO ⊨

RE-LACE the shoes using two skinny silk or chiffon scarves.

⊨ STEP THREE ⊨

ALLOW enough length at the ends to tie a large fluffy bow.

➤➤ TIP *Pair this look with dark skinny jeans or opaque tights and a simple skirt. If matching the laces proves problematic, you can always mix-and-match different skinny scarves for a bolder look. If you don't own two skinny scarves long enough to complete the laces, tie the scarves into bows and attach them to the tops of the shoes with clips.*

the NoLita
Necklace

═╡ STEP ONE ╞═

SELECT three lightweight silk scarves of equal length and tie the ends together in a tight knot. Begin braiding the three scarves together.

═╡ STEP TWO ╞═

ONCE the scarves are braided together, loosen the end knot.

═╡ STEP THREE ╞═

TUCK the ends into the loosened knot and tighten.

═╡ STEP FOVR ╞═

SLIP the finished necklace over the head and fluff the braid out to the desired width. If the necklace doesn't fit over the head, loosen the knot and adjust accordingly.

➤➤ TIP *See the following pages for suggested variations.*

➤ Mix It Up: *The Park Avenue Necklace*

» Mix It Up: *The Tribeca Necklace*

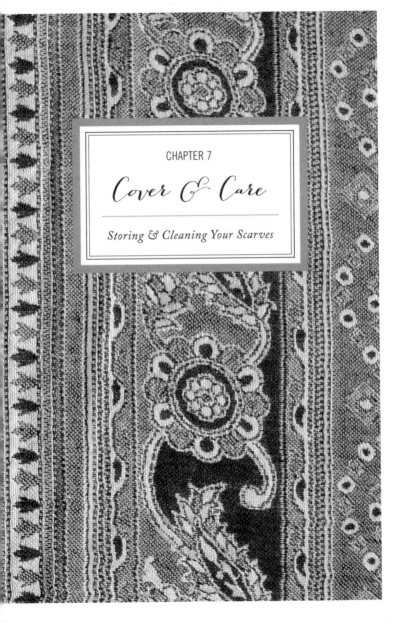

CHAPTER 7

Cover & Care

Storing & Cleaning Your Scarves

Caring for & Storing Your Scarves

Scarves can represent a significant wardrobe investment; a designer silk scarf can often compete with the price tag for a designer purse or pair of shoes. Additionally, many scarves are made out of delicate material—lace, chiffon, raw silk, light cashmere, to name a few—and easily tear if neglected or mishandled.

Delicate and expensive scarves require attention and care in order to ensure their longevity. Even scarves made of sturdier wool and machine-friendly cotton need a certain level of upkeep to keep them bright and ready to wear.

—General Care—

To hand-wash delicate items, fill a basin, bucket, or sink with slightly warm water and a detergent that has low alkaline (like Woolite) or even baby shampoo. Submerge the scarf and gently twirl underwater for two minutes, making sure the detergent or shampoo has dissipated in the water. Rinse the scarf by then submerging it in clean warm water—rinsing underneath a faucet could cause the material to stretch and fade. Spread the scarf on a large towel, making sure to not pull or stretch the scarf out of shape. Fold the towel over the scarf and press down to rid the scarf of excess water. Hang on a drying rack to let it air-dry (avoid hanging outdoors because the sun could cause color distortion).

CASHMERE: Although cashmere is generally delicate and made of natural fibers, this material is suitable for the dry cleaner. However, if the cashmere scarf is lightweight, it's best to hand-wash as directed above.

WOOL: Wool should generally be dry-cleaned or hand-washed in cold water. When hand-washing, wool can sit submerged in water for up to ten minutes. You may also squeeze woolen scarves gently to rid them of excess water, but do not wring or twist (this will break up the fiber and misshape the scarf).

SILK AND RAW SILK: Hand-wash as directed above, but use cold water. To restore shine to faded silk scarves, add vinegar to warm water (1 to 4 ratio) and hand-wash. Only iron on a silk setting, otherwise you might burn the material.

POLYESTER/SYNTHETIC BLENDS: Artificial materials like nylon, rayon, or polyester are generally suited for the washing machine. Use a lingerie bag and a mild detergent in cool water and run on the gentlest, shortest cycle possible. Dry on a cool cycle for five to ten minutes.

COTTON: Most cotton is fine to clean in a washing machine with cold water, but make sure to choose a color-safe detergent to prevent fading and air dry to avoid shrinking.

—General Storage—

Storing your scarves properly is almost as important as cleaning them. In order to keep your scarves undamaged and wrinkle-free, keep them rolled in a specific drawer or bin. However, scarves provide so much color, it's often hard to tuck them away in the back of the closet or underneath the bed. Here are just a few creative and utilitarian ways to store your scarves.

FOUR-TIERED HANGERS: You can find standard chrome and plastic four-tiered hangers at a local department or home-goods store. Drape your scarves on each of the tiers (depending on their width, it's possible to fit three to five scarves per row). Once this is complete, hang on the front of the closet door for additional color for your room.

BED POSTS: Loop and knot your scarves around the posts of the bed to keep them on display and accessorize your bed. Only use long scarves that won't be wrinkled or easily damaged.

DRAWERS: Roll each scarf and store in a chest of drawers or armoire. This method provides easy reference and ensures that your scarves are wrinkle-free. Add a lavender sachet or cedarwood chips to fend off moths and other pests (using mothballs will bring an unwelcome smell to your garments).

BINS & BOXES: In a plastic or cloth container, fold your scarves and place them in individual plastic bags. If you don't have plastic bags, include a lavender sachet or cedarwood chips.

—Brands Featured—

Admire & Covet

—Resources—

ALTER
109 Franklin St.
Brooklyn, NY 11222
*http://alterbrooklyn.blogspot
.com/p/online-store.html*

BARNEYS NEW YORK
660 Madison Avenue
New York, NY 10065
www.barneys.com

HELEN DEALTRY DESIGNS
*www.wokinggirldesigns
.myshopify.com*

ILANA KOHN
http://ilanakohn.com

LAUREN MANOOGIAN
http://laurenmanoogian.com

LEAH REENA GOREN
http://leahgoren.com

LOOPY MANGO
78 Grand St.
New York, NY 10013
www.loopymango.com

OUTLIER
87 Richardson St.
Brooklyn, NY 11211
http://outlier.cc

SAKS FIFTH AVENUE
611 5th Avenue
New York, New York 10022
www.saksfifthavenue.com

SHABD SIMON-ALEXANDER
http://shabdismyname.com